T0314488

BEYOND VIETNAM:
A TIME TO
BREAK SILENCE

DR.

MARTIN

LUTHER

KING JR.

———

BEYOND VIETNAM:
A TIME TO
BREAK SILENCE

Foreword by Viet Thanh Nguyen

**MartinLuther
KingJr.***Library*

**MartinLuther
KingJr.**_Library_

"Beyond Vietnam" reprinted by arrangement with The Heirs to the
Estate of Martin Luther King Jr., c/o Writers House as the proprietor,
New York, NY. Copyright © 1963 Dr. Martin Luther King Jr. © renewed
1991 Coretta Scott King.

Foreword Copyright © 2024 by Viet Thanh Nguyen

BEYOND VIETNAM. Copyright © 2024 by The Estate of Martin Luther
King, Jr. All rights reserved. Printed in the United States of America. No
part of this book may be used or reproduced in any manner whatsoever
without written permission except in the case of brief quotations
embodied in critical articles and reviews. For information, address
HarperCollins Publishers, 195 Broadway, New York, NY 10007.

In Association With

License granted by Intellectual Properties Management, Inc., Atlanta,
GA, exclusive licensor of The King Estate.

HarperCollins books may be purchased for educational, business, or
sales promotional use. For information, please email the Special Markets
Department at SPsales@harpercollins.com.

Designed by Ralph Fowler
Art © RZK Studio/Shutterstock

Library of Congress Cataloging-in-Publication Data has been applied for.

ISBN 978-0-06-335103-5

23 24 25 26 27 LBC 5 4 3 2 1

Foreword

"Beyond Vietnam" is an essay, a speech, and a prophecy. As an essay, it should be read. As a speech, it must be listened to. As a prophecy, it demands to be heard. But more than half a century after Martin Luther King Jr. wrote and delivered "Beyond Vietnam" at New York City's Riverside Church, have his words been heeded?

The context was 1967. The American war in Việt Nam was nearing its bloodiest peak, with more than half a million American soldiers soon to be serving in the country. Americans could watch images of death and destruction on their televisions over dinner. Thousands of American soldiers had died, as had tens of thousands, perhaps hundreds of thousands, of Vietnamese on all sides. Antiwar protests shook the nation, while a generation of young men was subjected to the draft.

His audience, King said, was first and foremost his fellow Americans. This was not to absolve others of their responsibility in the waging of war and the search for peace, most notably the Vietnamese themselves on all sides, caught up in both a civil war and a revolution. As an American, however, King wanted to address the political and moral culpability of his country, "the greatest purveyor of violence in the world today."

Amid a nation divided, King was both a hero and

an enemy. The FBI was surveilling and attempting to blackmail him, with J. Edgar Hoover, the FBI's director, believing King to be a subversive, perhaps even a communist. But King had also won the Nobel Peace Prize in 1964 for his civil rights activism. He felt "compelled to see the war as an enemy of the poor," with young Black men being sent to "guarantee liberties in Southeast Asia which they had not found in southwest Georgia and East Harlem."

If King had focused purely on the domestic effects of the war on Black Americans, his stance would still have been controversial, but probably less so than what would be manifest in "Beyond Vietnam." Like the boxer Muhammad Ali, who refused to be drafted on the grounds that the enemy of Black Americans was white Americans rather than the Vietnamese, King connected the racial and class inequities of American society to the racist conduct of the American war in Việt Nam. Even more radically, King argued that the war was an expression of capitalist greed, with the United States making "peaceful revolution impossible by refusing to give up the privileges and the pleasures that come from the immense profits of overseas investments."

Despite his critique of capitalism, King was not a communist. But he was also not the kind of anticommunist who saw the so-called cold war—which burned very hot for many Asians, Africans, and Latin Americans—as an apocalyptic conflict. In this clash between good and evil, only two choices could be made: us or them. It was thus that Black Americans who chose the United States' side, or who were drafted into it, found themselves standing shoulder to shoulder with white Americans "in brutal solidarity" against the Vietnamese.

King refused this moral peril and articulated a greater vision of global, peaceful solidarity. He understood the specificities and complexities of Vietnamese and Americans but located them in relationship to each other and to many others. When it came to recognizing the other who was also the enemy, real or perceived, King called for "compassion and nonviolence," hallmarks of his civil rights struggle. But he also saw that the place of Black Americans when it came to the war in Việt Nam was perhaps more treacherous than where they stood relative to civil rights. In the struggle against white supremacy, Black Americans demanded to have their voices heard, but when it came to the war, the Vietnamese became the "voiceless ones" for Americans, Black or white.

I imagine that King would have agreed with the writer and activist Arundhati Roy, who argued many years later that "there's really no such thing as the 'voiceless' . . . only the deliberately silenced or the preferably unheard." Indeed, King believed that the West's arrogance in "feeling that it has everything to teach others and nothing to learn from them" is "not just." He worked to hear and learn from the Vietnamese, as symbolized in his relationship to the vocal Buddhist monk and activist Thích Nhất Hạnh. King nominated him for the Nobel Peace Prize a few months before delivering "Beyond Vietnam" and two years after Thích Nhất Hạnh had written to King, encouraging him to take an anti-war stance. When King eventually wrote his speech, he subtitled it "A Time to Break Silence."

Breaking this silence around the war risked damaging King's civil rights cause, and indeed some of his civil rights colleagues opposed his taking such a public stance. But King's vision of peace and justice exceeded American boundaries, and he saw how the American war was not only slaughtering Vietnamese innocents but was also destroying whatever American innocence remained after centuries of settler colonialism, slavery, and wars of expansion. "If America's soul becomes totally poisoned," he said, "part of the autopsy must read: Vietnam." He spoke as a Black man, an American, and a citizen of the world, and as a reverend, a preacher, and a prophet with his eyes on the Divine who knew that the consequences of silence would be devastating for all Americans, white and Black and every shade in between, as well as for many others around the world.

"The war in Vietnam is but a symptom of a far deeper malady within the American spirit, and if we ignore this sobering reality," he said, "we will find ourselves organizing 'clergy and laymen concerned' committees for the next generation. They will be concerned about Guatemala . . . and Peru. They will be concerned about Thailand and Cambodia. They will be concerned about Mozambique and South Africa. We will be marching for these and a dozen other names and attending rallies without end, unless there is a significant and profound change in American life and policy."

King's prophecy has been borne out by the course of American foreign policy through the late twentieth and early twenty-first centuries, marked by cruel interventions in Central America and pointless and tragic wars in Iraq and Afghanistan. Although the American defeat in Việt Nam discouraged American adventurism for a couple of decades, the United States ultimately appears to have learned the wrong lessons.

While King's vital spirit and passion live on for many, it seems that, as a whole, we as a nation have not learned "the basic weaknesses of our own condition." I suspect that the majority of Americans have never even heard of "Beyond Vietnam," preferring instead the optimism of his most famous speech, "I Have a Dream." And yet if Americans were to read only one text by an American about the war in Việt Nam, I would recommend this one above all.

King declaimed "Beyond Vietnam" on April 4, 1967. On April 4, 1968, he was assassinated. He had fallen victim to the American violence that he had protested against and to which he had borne stubborn, courageous witness. That violence was and is endemic to the United States, arising from its origins in genocide, warfare, and enslavement. That violence succeeded in killing him, but it failed to silence him.

"We still have a choice today," he said. "Nonviolent coexistence or violent coannihilation." His day is still our day, his past continues into our present, and his challenge remains: "The choice is ours, and though we might prefer it otherwise, we must choose in this crucial moment of human history."

King chose and spoke out. Shall we?

—Viet Thanh Nguyen

"BEYOND VIETNAM: A TIME TO BREAK SILENCE" SPEECH

April 4, 1967
Riverside Church
New York City

Mr. Chairman,
ladies and gentlemen:

I need not pause to say how very delighted I am to be here tonight, and how very delighted I am to see you expressing your concern about the issues that will be discussed tonight by turning out in such large numbers.

I also want to say that I consider it a
great honor to share this program
with Dr. Bennett, Dr. Commager, and
Rabbi Heschel, and some of
the distinguished leaders and
personalities of our nation.

And of course it's always good to
come back to Riverside Church.

Over the last eight years, I have had the privilege of preaching here almost every year in that period, and it is always a rich and rewarding experience to come to this great church and this great pulpit.

I come to this magnificent house of worship tonight because my conscience leaves me no other choice.

I join you in this meeting because I'm in deepest agreement with the aims and work of the organization which has brought us together: Clergy and Laymen Concerned About Vietnam.

The recent statements of your executive committee are the sentiments of my own heart, and I found myself in full accord when I read its opening lines:

"A time comes when silence is betrayal." And that time has come for us in relation to Vietnam.

The truth of these words is beyond doubt, but the mission to which they call us is a most difficult one.

Even when pressed by the demands of inner truth, men do not easily assume the task of opposing their government's policy, especially in time of war.

Nor does the human spirit move without great difficulty against all the apathy of conformist thought within one's own bosom and in the surrounding world.

Moreover, when the issues at hand seem as perplexing as they often do in the case of this dreadful conflict, we are always on the verge of being mesmerized by uncertainty.

But we must move on.

And some of us who have already
begun to break the silence of
the night have found that the calling
to speak is often a vocation of agony,
but we must speak.

We must speak with all the humility
that is appropriate to our limited vision,
but we must speak.

And we must rejoice as well,
for surely this is the first time in our
nation's history that a significant
number of its religious leaders have
chosen to move beyond the prophesying
of smooth patriotism to the high
grounds of a firm dissent based upon
the mandates of conscience and the
reading of history.

Perhaps a new spirit is
rising among us.

If it is, let us trace its movements
and pray that our own inner being
may be sensitive to its guidance,
for we are deeply in need of a
new way beyond the darkness that
seems so close around us.

Over the past two years,
as I have moved to break the
betrayal of my own silences and to
speak from the burnings of
my own heart, as I have called
for radical departures from the
destruction of Vietnam,
many persons have questioned me
about the wisdom of my path.

At the heart of their concerns

this query has often loomed large

and loud: "Why are you speaking

about the war, Dr. King?"

"Why are you joining the

voices of dissent?"

"Peace and civil rights don't mix,"

they say.

"Aren't you hurting the cause of

your people?" they ask.

And when I hear them, though I often
understand the source of their concern,
I am nevertheless greatly saddened,
for such questions mean that the
inquirers have not really known me, my
commitment, or my calling.

Indeed, their questions suggest
that they do not know the world
in which they live.

In the light of such tragic misunderstanding, I deem it of signal importance to try to state clearly, and I trust concisely, why I believe that the path from Dexter Avenue Baptist Church—the church in Montgomery, Alabama, where I began my pastorate—leads clearly to this sanctuary tonight.

I come to this platform tonight
to make a passionate plea to
my beloved nation.

This speech is not addressed
to Hanoi or to the National
Liberation Front.

It is not addressed to
China or to Russia.

Nor is it an attempt to overlook the ambiguity of the total situation and the need for a collective solution to the tragedy of Vietnam.

Neither is it an attempt to make North Vietnam or the National Liberation Front paragons of virtue, nor to overlook the role they must play in the successful resolution of the problem.

While they both may have
justifiable reasons to be suspicious
of the good faith of the United States,
life and history give eloquent testimony
to the fact that conflicts are never
resolved without trustful
give-and-take on both sides.

Tonight, however, I wish not to
speak with Hanoi and the National
Liberation Front, but rather to
my fellow Americans.

Since I am a preacher by calling,
I suppose it is not surprising
that I have seven major reasons
for bringing Vietnam into the
field of my moral vision.

There is at the outset a very
obvious and almost facile connection
between the war in Vietnam
and the struggle I, and others, have
been waging in America.

A few years ago there was a shining
moment in that struggle.

It seemed as if there was a
real promise of hope for the poor—
both Black and white—through
the poverty program.

There were experiments,
hopes, new beginnings.

Then came the buildup in Vietnam, and I watched this program broken and eviscerated, as if it were some idle political plaything of a society gone mad on war, and I knew that America would never invest the necessary funds or energies in rehabilitation of its poor so long as adventures like Vietnam continued to draw men and skills and money like some demonic destructive suction tube.

So, I was increasingly compelled to see the war as an enemy of the poor and to attack it as such.

Perhaps a more tragic recognition of reality took place when it became clear to me that the war was doing far more than devastating the hopes of the poor at home.

It was sending their sons and
their brothers and their husbands
to fight and to die in extraordinarily
high proportions relative to the
rest of the population.

We were taking the Black young men
who had been crippled by our society
and sending them eight thousand
miles away to guarantee liberties
in Southeast Asia which they
had not found in southwest
Georgia and East Harlem.

And so we have been repeatedly
faced with the cruel irony of watching
Negro and white boys on TV screens as
they kill and die together for a nation
that has been unable to seat them
together in the same schools.

And so we watch them in brutal solidarity burning the huts of a poor village, but we realize that they would hardly live on the same block in Chicago.

I could not be silent in the face of such cruel manipulation of the poor.

My third reason moves to an even deeper level of awareness, for it grows out of my experience in the ghettos of the North over the last three years— especially the last three summers.

As I have walked among the desperate, rejected, and angry young men, I have told them that Molotov cocktails and rifles would not solve their problems.

I have tried to offer them my deepest

compassion while maintaining

my conviction that social change

comes most meaningfully through

nonviolent action.

But they ask—and rightly so—

what about Vietnam?

They ask if our own nation wasn't
using massive doses of violence
to solve its problems, to bring about
the changes it wanted.

Their questions hit home, and I
knew that I could never again raise
my voice against the violence of the
oppressed in the ghettos without having
first spoken clearly to the greatest
purveyor of violence in the world
today—my own government.

For the sake of those boys, for the sake of this government, for the sake of the hundreds of thousands trembling under our violence, I cannot be silent.

For those who ask the question,
"Aren't you a civil rights leader?"
and thereby mean to exclude me
from the movement for peace,
I have this further answer.

In 1957 when a group of us formed
the Southern Christian Leadership
Conference, we chose as our motto:
"To save the soul of America."

We were convinced that we could not limit our vision to certain rights for Black people, but instead affirmed the conviction that America would never be free or saved from itself until the descendants of its slaves were loosed completely from the shackles they still wear.

In a way we were agreeing with Langston Hughes, that Black bard of Harlem, who had written earlier:

O, yes,

I say it plain,

America never was America to me,

And yet I swear this oath—

America will be!

Now, it should be incandescently clear that no one who has any concern for the integrity and life of America today can ignore the present war.

If America's soul becomes totally poisoned, part of the autopsy must read: Vietnam.

It can never be saved so long

as it destroys the deepest hopes

of men the world over.

So it is that those of us who are

yet determined that America will

be—are—are led down the path

of protest and dissent, working

for the health of our land.

As if the weight of such a
commitment to the life and health
of America were not enough, another
burden of responsibility was
placed upon me in 1954.*

---

* King stated "1954." That year was notable for the Civil Rights Movement in the USSC's Brown v. Board of Education ruling. However, given the statement's discursive thrust, King may have meant to say "1964"—the year he won the Nobel Peace Prize. Alternatively, as noted by Steve Goldberg, King may have identified 1954's "burden of responsibility" as the year he became a minister.

And I cannot forget that the
Nobel Peace Prize was also a
commission, a commission to work
harder than I had ever worked before
for "the brotherhood of man."

This is a calling that takes me beyond
national allegiances, but even if it
were not present I would yet have to
live with the meaning of my
commitment to the ministry
of Jesus Christ.

To me the relationship of this ministry
to the making of peace is so obvious
that I sometimes marvel at those
who ask me why I'm speaking
against the war.

Could it be that they do not know
that the good news was meant for
all men—for Communist and capitalist,
for their children and ours, for Black
and for white, for revolutionary
and conservative?

Have they forgotten that my
ministry is in obedience to the
One who loved his enemies so
fully that he died for them?

What then can I say to the Vietcong
or to Castro or to Mao as a faithful
minister of this One?

Can I threaten them with death or must
I not share with them my life?

And finally, as I try to explain
for you and for myself the road that
leads from Montgomery to this
place, I would have offered all that was
most valid if I simply said that I
must be true to my conviction that I
share with all men the calling to be a
son of the living God.

Beyond the calling of race or nation
or creed is this vocation of sonship
and brotherhood, and because
I believe that the Father is deeply
concerned especially for his suffering
and helpless and outcast children,
I come tonight to speak for them.

This I believe to be the privilege
and the burden of all of us who deem
ourselves bound by allegiances and
loyalties which are broader and deeper
than nationalism and which
go beyond our nation's self-defined
goals and positions.

We are called to speak for the weak,
for the voiceless, for the victims of our
nation, and for those it calls "enemy,"
for no document from human
hands can make these humans any
less our brothers.

And as I ponder the madness of
Vietnam and search within myself for
ways to understand and respond in
compassion, my mind goes constantly to
the people of that peninsula.

I speak now not of the soldiers

of each side, not of the ideologies of

the Liberation Front, not of the

junta in Saigon, but simply of

the people who have been living

under the curse of war for almost three

continuous decades now.

I think of them, too, because it is
clear to me that there will be no
meaningful solution there until some
attempt is made to know them
and hear their broken cries.

They must see Americans
as strange liberators.

The Vietnamese people proclaimed
their own independence in 1954—
in 1945, rather—after a combined
French and Japanese occupation
and before the Communist
revolution in China.

They were led by Ho Chi Minh.

Even though they quoted the

American Declaration of Independence

in their own document of freedom,

we refused to recognize them.

Instead, we decided to support

France in its reconquest of

her former colony.

Our government felt then that the Vietnamese people were not ready for independence, and we again fell victim to the deadly Western arrogance that has poisoned the international atmosphere for so long.

With that tragic decision we rejected a revolutionary government seeking self-determination and a government that had been established not by China— for whom the Vietnamese have no great love—but by clearly indigenous forces that included some Communists.

For the peasants this new government meant real land reform, one of the most important needs in their lives.

For nine years following 1945 we
denied the people of Vietnam the
right of independence.

For nine years we vigorously supported
the French in their abortive effort to
recolonize Vietnam.

Before the end of the war we
were meeting eighty percent of
the French war costs.

Even before the French were
defeated at Dien Bien Phu, they
began to despair of their reckless
action, but we did not.

We encouraged them with our huge
financial and military supplies to
continue the war even after
they had lost the will.

Soon we would be paying almost the
full costs of this tragic attempt
at recolonization.

After the French were defeated, it
looked as if independence and land
reform would come again through
the Geneva Agreement.

But instead there came the United States, determined that Ho should not unify the temporarily divided nation, and the peasants watched again as we supported one of the most vicious modern dictators, our chosen man, Premier Diem.

The peasants watched and cringed as Diem ruthlessly rooted out all opposition, supported their extortionist landlords, and refused even to discuss reunification with the North.

The peasants watched as all this was presided over by United States' influence and then by increasing numbers of United States troops who came to help quell the insurgency that Diem's methods had aroused.

When Diem was overthrown they
may have been happy, but the long
line of military dictators seemed to offer
no real change, especially in terms of
their need for land and peace.

The only change came from America,
as we increased our troop commitments
in support of governments which
were singularly corrupt, inept, and
without popular support.

All the while the people read our
leaflets and received the regular
promises of peace and democracy
and land reform.

Now they languish under our bombs
and consider us, not their fellow
Vietnamese, the real enemy.

They move sadly and apathetically
as we herd them off the land of their
fathers into concentration camps where
minimal social needs are rarely met.

They know they must move on or be
destroyed by our bombs.

So they go, primarily women and

children and the aged.

They watch as we poison their

water, as we kill a million acres

of their crops.

They must weep as the bulldozers

roar through their areas preparing

to destroy the precious trees.

They wander into the hospitals
with at least twenty casualties from
American firepower for one
Vietcong-inflicted injury.

So far we may have killed a million
of them, mostly children.

They wander into the towns and see

thousands of the children, homeless,

without clothes, running in packs on

the streets like animals.

They see the children degraded

by our soldiers as they beg for food.

They see the children selling

their sisters to our soldiers,

soliciting for their mothers.

What do the peasants think as we ally
ourselves with the landlords and as we
refuse to put any action into our many
words concerning land reform?

What do they think as we test out
our latest weapons on them,
just as the Germans tested out new
medicine and new tortures in the
concentration camps of Europe?

Where are the roots of the independent
Vietnam we claim to be building?

Is it among these voiceless ones?

We have destroyed their two most
cherished institutions: the family
and the village.

We have destroyed their land
and their crops.

We have cooperated in the crushing—
in the crushing of the nation's only
non-Communist revolutionary political
force, the Unified Buddhist Church.

We have supported the enemies
of the peasants of Saigon.

We have corrupted their women and
children and killed their men.

Now there is little left to build on,
save bitterness.

Soon, the only solid—solid physical
foundations remaining will be found at
our military bases and in the concrete
of the concentration camps we call
"fortified hamlets."

The peasants may well wonder if
we plan to build our new Vietnam
on such grounds as these.

Could we blame them for

such thoughts?

We must speak for them and raise

the questions they cannot raise.

These, too, are our brothers.

Perhaps a more difficult but
no less necessary task is to speak
for those who have been
designated as our enemies.

What of the National Liberation
Front, that strangely anonymous group
we call "VC" or "Communists"?

What must they think of the United States of America when they realize that we permitted the repression and cruelty of Diem, which helped to bring them into being as a resistance group in the South?

What do they think of our condoning the violence which led to their own taking up of arms?

How can they believe in our integrity
when now we speak of "aggression
from the North" as if there were
nothing more essential to the war?

How can they trust us when now
we charge them with violence
after the murderous reign of Diem
and charge them with violence while
we pour every new weapon of
death into their land?

Surely we must understand
their feelings, even if we do not
condone their actions.

Surely we must see that the
men we supported pressed them
to their violence.

Surely we must see that our own
computerized plans of destruction
simply dwarf their greatest acts.

How do they judge us when our
officials know that their membership
is less than twenty-five percent
Communist, and yet insist on giving
them the blanket name?

What must they be thinking

when they know that we are aware

of their control of major sections of

Vietnam, and yet we appear ready to

allow national elections in which this

highly organized political parallel

government will not have a part?

They ask how we can speak of
free elections when the Saigon press
is censored and controlled by the
military junta.

And they are surely right to
wonder what kind of new
government we plan to help form
without them, the only party in real
touch with the peasants.

They question our political goals
and they deny the reality of a
peace settlement from which
they will be excluded.

Their questions are
frighteningly relevant.

Is our nation planning to build on political myth again, and then shore it up upon the power of new violence?

Here is the true meaning and value of compassion and nonviolence, when it helps us to see the enemy's point of view, to hear his questions, to know his assessment of ourselves.

For from his view we may indeed
see the basic weaknesses of our own
condition, and if we are mature, we
may learn and grow and profit from
the wisdom of the brothers who
are called the opposition.

So, too, with Hanoi. In the North, where our bombs now pummel the land, and our mines endanger the waterways, we are met by a deep but understandable mistrust.

To speak for them is to explain this lack of confidence in Western words, and especially their distrust of American intentions now.

In Hanoi are the men who led the nation to independence against the Japanese and the French, the men who sought membership in the French Commonwealth and were betrayed by the weakness of Paris and the willfulness of the colonial armies.

It was they who led a second struggle against French domination at tremendous costs, and then were persuaded to give up the land they controlled between the thirteenth and seventeenth parallel as a temporary measure at Geneva.

After 1954 they watched us conspire

with Diem to prevent elections which

could have surely brought Ho Chi Minh

to power over a united Vietnam,

and they realized they had been

betrayed again.

When we ask why they do not

leap to negotiate, these things

must be remembered.

Also, it must be clear that the leaders of Hanoi considered the presence of American troops in support of the Diem regime to have been the initial military breach of the Geneva Agreement concerning foreign troops.

They remind us that they did not
begin to send troops in large numbers
and even supplies into the South
until American forces had moved
into the tens of thousands.

Hanoi remembers how our
leaders refused to tell us the truth
about the earlier North Vietnamese
overtures for peace, how the president
claimed that none existed when
they had clearly been made.

Ho Chi Minh has watched as America has spoken of peace and built up its forces, and now he has surely heard the increasing international rumors of American plans for an invasion of the North.

He knows the bombing and shelling and mining we are doing are part of traditional pre-invasion strategy.

Perhaps only his sense of humor

and of irony can save him when he

hears the most powerful nation

of the world speaking of aggression

as it drops thousands of bombs on

a poor, weak nation more than

eight hundred—rather, eight thousand

miles away from its shores.

At this point I should make it clear that while I have tried in these last few minutes to give a voice to the voiceless in Vietnam and to understand the arguments of those who are called "enemy," I am as deeply concerned about our own troops there as anything else.

For it occurs to me that what we are submitting them to in Vietnam is not simply the brutalizing process that goes on in any war where armies face each other and seek to destroy.

We are adding cynicism to the process of death, for they must know after a short period there that none of the things we claim to be fighting for are really involved.

Before long they must know that
their government has sent them
into a struggle among Vietnamese,
and the more sophisticated surely
realize that we are on the side of the
wealthy, and the secure, while
we create a hell for the poor.

Somehow this madness must cease.

We must stop now.

I speak as a child of God and
brother to the suffering poor
of Vietnam.

I speak for those whose land is
being laid waste, whose homes are
being destroyed, whose culture
is being subverted.

I speak of the—for the poor of
America who are paying the double
price of smashed hopes at home, and
death and corruption in Vietnam.

I speak as a citizen of the world,
for the world as it stands aghast
at the path we have taken.

I speak as one who loves America, to

the leaders of our own nation:

The great initiative in this war is ours;

the initiative to stop it must be ours.

This is the message of the great

Buddhist leaders of Vietnam.

Recently one of them wrote these words, and I quote:

"Each day the war goes on the hatred increases in the heart of the Vietnamese and in the hearts of those of humanitarian instinct.

"The Americans are forcing even their friends into becoming their enemies.

"It is curious that the Americans, who calculate so carefully on the possibilities of military victory, do not realize that in the process they are incurring deep psychological and political defeat.

"The image of America will never again be the image of revolution, freedom, and democracy, but the image of violence and militarism."

If we continue, there will be no doubt in my mind and in the mind of the world that we have no honorable intentions in Vietnam.

If we do not stop our war against the people of Vietnam immediately, the world will be left with no other alternative than to see this as some horrible, clumsy, and deadly game we have decided to play.

The world now demands a maturity
of America that we may not be
able to achieve.

It demands that we admit that
we have been wrong from the
beginning of our adventure in
Vietnam, that we have been
detrimental to the life of the
Vietnamese people.

The situation is one in which we
must be ready to turn sharply
from our present ways.

In order to atone for our sins
and errors in Vietnam, we should
take the initiative in bringing
a halt to this tragic war.

I would like to suggest five concrete things that our government should do to begin the long and difficult process of extricating ourselves from this nightmarish conflict:

Number one: End all bombing in North and South Vietnam.

Number two: Declare a unilateral
cease-fire in the hope that such action
will create the atmosphere
for negotiation.

Three: Take immediate steps to
prevent other battlegrounds in
Southeast Asia by curtailing our
military buildup in Thailand and our
interference in Laos.

Four: Realistically accept the fact that the National Liberation Front has substantial support in South Vietnam and must thereby play a role in any meaningful negotiations and any future Vietnam government.

Five: Set a date that we will remove all foreign troops from Vietnam in accordance with the 1954 Geneva Agreement.

Part of our ongoing—Part of our

ongoing commitment might well

express itself in an offer to grant asylum

to any Vietnamese who fears for

his life under a new regime which

included the Liberation Front.

Then we must make what reparations

we can for the damage we have done.

We must provide the medical aid
that is badly needed, making it available
in this country, if necessary.

Meanwhile, we in the churches
and synagogues have a continuing
task while we urge our government
to disengage itself from a disgraceful
commitment.

We must continue to raise our voices and our lives if our nation persists in its perverse ways in Vietnam.

We must be prepared to match actions with words by seeking out every creative method of protest possible.

As we counsel young men concerning military service, we must clarify for them our nation's role in Vietnam and challenge them with the alternative of conscientious objection.

I am pleased to say that this is a path
now chosen by more than seventy
students at my own alma mater,
Morehouse College, and I recommend
it to all who find the American
course in Vietnam a dishonorable
and unjust one.

Moreover, I would encourage
all ministers of draft age to give up
their ministerial exemptions and seek
status as conscientious objectors.

These are the times for real
choices and not false ones.

We are at the moment when our lives must be placed on the line if our nation is to survive its own folly.

Every man of humane convictions must decide on the protest that best suits his convictions, but we must all protest.

Now there is something seductively tempting about stopping there and sending us all off on what in some circles has become a popular crusade against the war in Vietnam.

I say we must enter that struggle, but I wish to go on now to say something even more disturbing.

The war in Vietnam is but a
symptom of a far deeper malady within
the American spirit, and if we ignore
this sobering reality—and if we ignore
this sobering reality, we will
find ourselves organizing "clergy and
laymen concerned" committees
for the next generation.

They will be concerned about
Guatemala—Guatemala and Peru.

They will be concerned about
Thailand and Cambodia.

They will be concerned about
Mozambique and South Africa.

We will be marching for these and a
dozen other names and attending
rallies without end, unless there is a
significant and profound change in
American life and policy.

And so, such thoughts take us beyond
Vietnam, but not beyond our calling
as sons of the living God.

In 1957, a sensitive American official overseas said that it seemed to him that our nation was on the wrong side of a world revolution.

During the past ten years, we have seen emerge a pattern of suppression which has now justified the presence of US military advisors in Venezuela.

This need to maintain social stability
for our investments accounts for
the counterrevolutionary action of
American forces in Guatemala.

It tells why American helicopters
are being used against guerrillas in
Cambodia and why American napalm
and Green Beret forces have already
been active against rebels in Peru.

It is with such activity in mind that
the words of the late John F. Kennedy
come back to haunt us.

Five years ago he said,
"Those who make peaceful revolution
impossible will make violent
revolution inevitable."

Increasingly, by choice or by accident, this is the role our nation has taken, the role of those who make peaceful revolution impossible by refusing to give up the privileges and the pleasures that come from the immense profits of overseas investments.

I am convinced that if we are to get

on the right side of the world revolution,

we as a nation must undergo a

radical revolution of values.

We must rapidly begin—

We must rapidly begin the shift

from a thing-oriented society to a

person-oriented society.

When machines and computers,
profit motives and property rights,
are considered more important than
people, the giant triplets of racism,
extreme materialism, and militarism are
incapable of being conquered.

A true revolution of values will
soon cause us to question the fairness
and justice of many of our past
and present policies.

On the one hand, we are called to play the Good Samaritan on life's roadside, but that will be only an initial act.

One day we must come to see that the whole Jericho Road must be transformed so that men and women will not be constantly beaten and robbed as they make their journey on life's highway.

True compassion is more than
flinging a coin to a beggar.

It comes to see that an
edifice which produces beggars
needs restructuring.

A true revolution of values will soon
look uneasily on the glaring contrast
of poverty and wealth.

With righteous indignation, it will look across the seas and see individual capitalists of the West investing huge sums of money in Asia, Africa, and South America, only to take the profits out with no concern for the social betterment of the countries, and say, "This is not just."

It will look at our alliance with the
landed gentry of South America
and say, "This is not just."

The Western arrogance of feeling that
it has everything to teach others and
nothing to learn from them is not just.

A true revolution of values will lay
hand on the world order and say
of war, "This way of settling
differences is not just."

This business of burning human beings with napalm, of filling our nation's homes with orphans and widows, of injecting poisonous drugs of hate into the veins of peoples normally humane, of sending men home from dark and bloody battlefields physically handicapped and psychologically deranged, cannot be reconciled with wisdom, justice, and love.

A nation that continues year after
year to spend more money on military
defense than on programs of social
uplift is approaching spiritual death.

America, the richest and most
powerful nation in the world,
can well lead the way in this
revolution of values.

There is nothing except a tragic death
wish to prevent us from reordering
our priorities so that the pursuit of
peace will take precedence over
the pursuit of war.

There is nothing to keep us
from molding a recalcitrant status
quo with bruised hands until we have
fashioned it into a brotherhood.

This kind of positive revolution
of values is our best defense
against Communism.

War is not the answer.

Communism will never be
defeated by the use of atomic bombs
or nuclear weapons.

Let us not join those who shout war and, through their misguided passions, urge the United States to relinquish its participation in the United Nations.

These are days which demand wise restraint and calm reasonableness.

We must not engage in a negative anti-Communism, but rather in a positive thrust for democracy, realizing that our greatest defense against Communism is to take offensive action in behalf of justice.

We must with positive action seek to remove those conditions of poverty, insecurity, and injustice, which are the fertile soil in which the seed of Communism grows and develops.

These are revolutionary times.

All over the globe men are revolting

against old systems of exploitation and

oppression, and out of the wounds

of a frail world, new systems of justice

and equality are being born.

The shirtless and barefoot people of the

land are rising up as never before.

"The people who sat in darkness

have seen a great light."*

We in the West must support

these revolutions.

---

* Isaiah 9:2/Matthew 4:16

It is a sad fact that because of comfort, complacency, a morbid fear of Communism, and our proneness to adjust to injustice, the Western nations that initiated so much of the revolutionary spirit of the modern world have now become the arch antirevolutionaries.

This has driven many to feel that only Marxism has a revolutionary spirit.

Therefore, Communism is a judgment against our failure to make democracy real and follow through on the revolutions that we initiated.

Our only hope today lies in our ability to recapture the revolutionary spirit and go out into a sometimes hostile world declaring eternal hostility to poverty, racism, and militarism.

With this powerful commitment we shall boldly challenge the status quo and unjust mores, and thereby speed the day when "every valley shall be exalted, and every mountain and hill shall be made low, and the crooked shall be made straight, and the rough places plain."[*]

* Isaiah 40:4

A genuine revolution of values means in the final analysis that our loyalties must become ecumenical rather than sectional.

Every nation must now develop an overriding loyalty to mankind as a whole in order to preserve the best in their individual societies.

This call for a worldwide fellowship that lifts neighborly concern beyond one's tribe, race, class, and nation is in reality a call for an all-embracing— embracing and unconditional love for all mankind.

This oft misunderstood, this oft misinterpreted concept, so readily dismissed by the Nietzsches of the world as a weak and cowardly force, has now become an absolute necessity for the survival of man.

When I speak of love I am not speaking of some sentimental and weak response.

I am not speaking of that force
which is just emotional bosh.

I am speaking of that force which all
of the great religions have seen as the
supreme unifying principle of life.

Love is somehow the key
that unlocks the door which leads
to ultimate reality.

This Hindu-Muslim-Christian-Jewish-
Buddhist belief about ultimate—
ultimate reality is beautifully summed
up in the first epistle of Saint John:

"Let us love one another,
for love is God. And every one that
loveth is born of God and knoweth
God. He that loveth not knoweth
not God, for God is love."

"If we love one another, God dwelleth in us and his love is perfected in us."*

Let us hope that this spirit will become the order of the day.

We can no longer afford to worship the god of hate or bow before the altar of retaliation.

---

* 1 John 4:7–8, 12

The oceans of history are made turbulent by the ever-rising tides of hate.

And history is cluttered with the wreckage of nations and individuals that pursued this self-defeating path of hate.

As Arnold Toynbee says:

"Love is the ultimate force

that makes for the saving choice of

life and good against the damning

choice of death and evil. Therefore

the first hope in our inventory must

be the hope that love is going to have

the last word."

We are now faced with the fact, my
friends, that tomorrow is today.

We are confronted with the
fierce urgency of now.

In this unfolding conundrum of life
and history, there is such a thing
as being too late.

Procrastination is still the thief of time.

Life often leaves us standing bare,
naked, and dejected with a lost
opportunity.

The tide in the affairs of men does not
remain at flood—it ebbs.

We may cry out desperately
for time to pause in her passage,
but time is adamant to every
plea and rushes on.

Over the bleached bones and jumbled residues of numerous civilizations are written the pathetic words, "Too late."

There is an invisible book of life that faithfully records our vigilance or our neglect.

Omar Khayyam is right:
"The moving finger writes, and
having writ moves on."

We still have a choice today:
nonviolent coexistence or violent
coannihilation.

We must move past
indecision to action.

We must find new ways to speak
for peace in Vietnam and justice
throughout the developing world, a
world that borders on our doors.

If we do not act, we shall surely be dragged down the long, dark, and shameful corridors of time reserved for those who possess power without compassion, might without morality, and strength without sight.

Now let us begin.

Now let us rededicate ourselves
to the long and bitter, but beautiful,
struggle for a new world.

This is the calling of the sons of God,
and our brothers wait eagerly
for our response.

Shall we say the odds are too great?

Shall we tell them the struggle
is too hard?

Will our message be that the forces of
American life militate against their
arrival as full men, and we send our
deepest regrets?

Or will there be another message—
of longing, of hope, of solidarity with
their yearnings, of commitment to their
cause, whatever the cost?

The choice is ours, and though
we might prefer it otherwise,
we must choose in this crucial
moment of human history.

As that noble bard of yesterday, James Russell Lowell, eloquently stated:

"Once to every man and nation comes
a moment to decide,

In the strife of Truth and Falsehood,
for the good or evil side;

Some great cause, God's new Messiah
offering each the bloom or blight,

And the choice goes by forever 'twixt that
darkness and that light.

"Though the cause of evil prosper,
yet 'tis truth alone is strong

Though her portions be the scaffold,
and upon the throne be wrong

Yet that scaffold sways the future,
and behind the dim unknown

Standeth God within the shadow,
keeping watch above his own."

And if we will only make the right choice, we will be able to transform this pending cosmic elegy into a creative psalm of peace.

If we will make the right choice, we will be able to transform the jangling discords of our world into a beautiful symphony of brotherhood.

If we will but make the right choice, we will be able to speed up the day, all over America and all over the world, when "justice will roll down like waters, and righteousness like a mighty stream."*

---

* Amos 5:24

About Martin Luther King Jr.

Dr. Martin Luther King Jr. (1929–1968), civil rights leader and recipient of the Nobel Prize for Peace, inspired and sustained the struggle for freedom, nonviolence, interracial brotherhood, and social justice.

About Viet Thanh Nguyen

Viet Thanh Nguyen is the author of the novel *The Sympathizer*, which won the Pulitzer Prize for Fiction, and its sequel, *The Committed*. His other books include *Nothing Ever Dies: Vietnam and the Memory of War*, a finalist for the National Book Award in General Nonfiction, and *A Man of Two Faces: A Memoir, A History, A Memorial*, as well as a collection of short stories, *The Refugees*.